Let's Go For A Walk

with **Ranger Hamza**

Illustrated by Kate Kronreif

ivy Kids

Hello, I'm Ranger Hamza.

Shall we go for a walk today?

Take this book with you, and let's have fun spotting things on our walk together.

Walking in the country, by the sea or in the town,

so many wonderful things to see if you stop to look around!

Open your eyes, open your ears, pause and take things in.

Let's pack our bags, get kitted out, and let the walk begin!

Let's go for a walk!

Roses are red, holly berries are too.
We're looking for RED things. Can you find a few?

Tomatoes and chilies, ripe apples and cherries.
Radishes and cranberries and juicy strawberries.
A shiny red bucket and a red swirly gate.

What red things will you spot on your walk today?

The colors of nature change throughout the year.

In spring and summer, red flowers come into bloom.

In fall, the leaves of some types of tree turn from green to red.

In winter, red berries on bushes feed hungry birds.

What RED things can you see where you are?

I spy something short,

I spy something tall.

I spy something **big**,

I spy something small.

Have a look around.
What is the tallest thing you can see?
Perhaps it is a building or a tree?

Plants come in many different sizes.

Some trees, like great oaks, can grow for many years to be very tall and big.

Some plants, like daisies, have flowers that only last one year and are very short and small.

What BIG and SMALL things can you spot?

How do things feel when we touch them with our hands?

Are they smooth like a pebble, or rough like sand?

Slimy like seaweed, or wet like the sea?

Hard like a rock, or soft like ice cream?

There are so many different textures to explore.

What TEXTURES can you find on your walk today?

A rough shell protects the oyster inside from crabs and seabirds that want to eat them.

Seaweed might be slimy but it's an important food source for many sea creatures.

Using a magnifying glass you can see that sand is made up of lots of little grains of different rocks and minerals.

What can we smell?
Let us use our noses.

Fresh fish?

Baking bread?

Bunches of roses?

Smoke from a chimney?

Slices of cheese?

Spices like pepper that make you sneeze!

Smells can be nice, and smells can be yucky.

Some strong cheeses smell like stinky feet!

Flowers like lavender have a nice smell to attract bees and other insects to collect their pollen.

What can you SMELL right now when you sniff the air?

The bridge is an arch,

the picnic rug's a square.

When you start to look,
you see shapes everywhere!

The boat sails are triangles,

the portholes are round.

Wherever you are walking
there are shapes to be found!

Portholes are covered windows in the side of a boat for letting in air and light.

Wind blows against the sails on a boat and pushes it through the water.

What different SHAPES can you spot on your walk?

Can you spot things that fly, like butterflies and bees?

Or wriggle like caterpillars
on leaves in the trees?

Slither slowly like snails
or scurry like ants?

Or crawl like beetles on rocks and on plants?

They are all small and often hiding away.

**How many BUGS can you find
on your walk today?**

A caterpillar eats lots of food to grow, then finds a safe spot to settle. It makes a hard shell, called a chrysalis or a cocoon. Inside the hard shell, the caterpillar transforms into a butterfly or moth.

A single ant can carry fifty times its own bodyweight.

SOUNDS are all around.

Birds tweeting.

Puddles splashing.

Leaves rustling.

Children chatting.

So many SOUNDS.
Open your ears. Listen carefully.
What can you hear?

Sounds are useful. People and animals use sounds to tell each other things.

Birds call to tell other birds "Here I am!" or "Danger—watch out!"

A bicycle bell warns other cyclists or pedestrians that you are coming through.

A B C and 1 2 3,
what letters and numbers can you see?

I spot a poster that says,
"Visit the zoo!"

And a bus
passing by,
number 32.

Can you spot any letters or numbers where you are?

Streets are given names so that they are easier to find.

A house number and street name together are called an address. We write the address on a letter or parcel we want to send.

Every building on a street is given a number or a name.

Everything looks different when it is dark.

We can gaze at the Moon and the twinkling stars.
We can make funny shadows appear on a wall,
and listen out for a distant owl's call.
Moths are fluttering around the light,
and the lamps on the truck are shining bright.

What can you spot on a walk at NIGHT?

Most owls are nocturnal.

This means they are active during the night and sleep during the day.

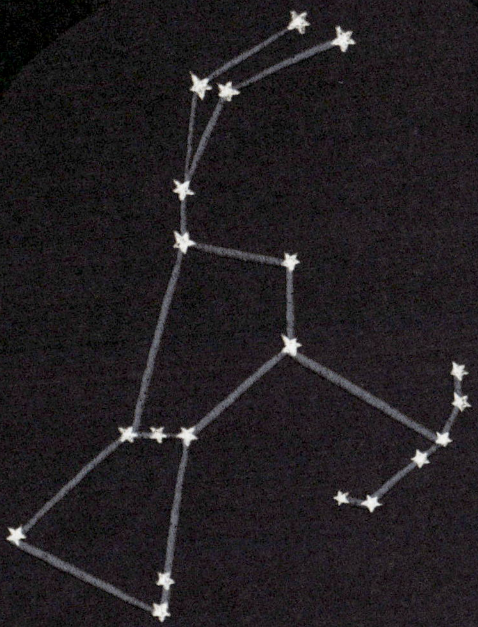

A constellation is a group of stars in the sky that make a pattern. This constellation is called Orion, and the three stars in the middle are called Orion's Belt.

Moths are attracted to man-made lights like streetlamps.

One, two. One, two.
I spy a pair of muddy boots.

Two bicycle wheels.

Two oars to row.

Two children swinging
to and fro.

Two ducks on the water.

Two squirrels in
the tree.

Two together is called a pair.
How many PAIRS can you see?

Ducks have a special oil gland near their tail that helps make their feathers waterproof.

Squirrels have long, bushy tails.

These help them to balance as they leap around the treetops.

Oars have a flat blade at one end. They are used to move and steer a boat through water.

What are things made of?
What materials can we spot?

A metal digger with rubber tires.
A ceramic flower pot.

A house built with bricks
and a wooden door.

Glass windows
to see through.

What are things made
of where you are?

**Can you spot
MATERIALS too?**

Some tires are made from natural rubber. The rubber is made from a liquid found inside certain trees.

Glass is made from melted sand—the same sand that you could find at the beach or in the desert.

Wood comes from the trunks and branches of trees. If you cut through the trunk of a tree, you can learn how many years old it is by counting the number of rings.

What can you spot when you look up high?

A cloud shaped like a rabbit.

A jet plane roaring by.

A bird's nest on the chimney pot.

A kite stuck in a tree.

Look up HIGH where you are.
What can you see?

There are different types of clouds.

Cumulus clouds are puffy and fluffy.

Stratus clouds look like a huge thick blanket covering the sky. These clouds are a good sign that rain is on the way.

Cirrus clouds are thin and wispy.

If it rains when the Sun is shining, you might see a rainbow.

What can we see when we
look
down?

A zig zag pattern
on the ground.

A crack in the
concrete with a flower
growing through.

Stripes in the grass, all
sparkly with dew.

An earthworm wriggling in the mud.

Crunchy leaves and pinecones
and daisies in bud.

While you're out on a walk
why not look at the GROUND?
There is so much to spot when you look DOWN.

Some plants can grow in the tiniest of cracks as long as they have sunlight and rain.

Earthworms have no eyes or ears, but they are very sensitive to vibrations.

Daisies close their petals at night and open them again in the morning.

It's like they are going to sleep!

Can you remember what you saw on your walk today?

Did you look up?

Did you look down?

Did you look all around?

Why not draw a map of the route you took today? And add in all the wonderful things you spotted along the way.

What did you hear?

What colors did you spot?

Did you notice any shapes?

What did you smell?

Did you count anything?

What did you touch?

Remember, every time you go for a walk, keep your eyes and ears open and you can always have

AN ADVENTURE!